MW01129200

Microwave

Mug Meals

Introduction

In our hectic busy lives, many people want a quick easy meal to eat on the go. We don't have time to cook big meals but we want something that is hot and fresh. The microwave is a great tool for heating up food quickly and easily. When food is microwaved in a mug it is a nice convenient way to take our food with us.

Whether we are in the office breakroom, in the college dorm room, a busy on the go singleton or just need a good meal fast, this cookbook has pages of delicious mouth-watering dishes. Quick and easy cooking has been elevated to a higher level with tasty mug meals for breakfast, lunch, snacks, dinner, and desserts.

Mug Coffee Cake

Ingredients:

1 tbsp. granulated sugar
2 1/2 tbsps. all-purpose flour
1/8 tsp. salt
1/4 tsp. baking powder
1 tbsp. vegetable oil or plain nonfat greek yogurt
1 tbsp. nonfat milk or almond milk
Dash of vanilla
1/2 tbsp. brown sugar
1/4 tsp. ground cinnamon

Directions:

1. Spray a mug or a ramekin with nonstick cooking spray.
2. Add sugar, flour, salt, baking powder, oil, milk, and vanilla and stir until combined.
3. Sprinkle brown sugar and cinnamon on top.
4. Microwave for about 45 seconds.
5. Enjoy warm!

Chocolate Mug Cake

Ingredients:

1/4 cup self-rising flour
1/4 cup Stevia
2 tbsp. cocoa
1/4 tsp. baking powder
1/8 tsp. salt
4.5 tbsp. milk
1 tbsp. coconut oil
3 tbsp. water
1/4 tsp. vanilla
2 tsp. mini chocolate chips
2 strawberries

Directions:

1. Begin by combining all your dry ingredients and pouring into a microwave-safe mug.
2. Add wet ingredients and mix until well combined.
3. Pour in 1 tsp. of mini chocolate chips.
4. Microwave on high for 1 minute and 45 seconds.
5. Top with remaining mini chips and strawberries.
6. Serve and enjoy!

Chocolate Chip Mug Cake

Ingredients:

2 tbsps. unsalted butter room temperature
1/4 cup plus 1 tbsp. all-purpose flour
1/4 cup dark brown sugar, not packed
2 tbsps. milk
1/2 tsp. baking powder
1 pinch salt + more for topping
2 1/2 tbsps. semi-sweet chocolate chips, plus more for topping

Directions:

1. Place butter in a large microwave safe coffee mug. Microwave until just melted (don't let get very hot) about 30- 60 seconds. (It melts faster in a wide mug and takes a bit longer in tall, narrow mug).
2. Remove mug from microwave and add flour, dark brown sugar, milk, baking powder and salt.
3. Stir well with a fork, until smooth.
4. Stir in 2 1/2 tbsps. chocolate chips.
5. Microwave (on high) for 1 minute and 25 seconds for a wide mug (as shown in the picture) or 1 minute and 35 seconds for a tall, narrow mug.
6. Remove from microwave, sprinkle more chocolate chips and.
7. Serve and enjoy!

Microwave Nutella Mug Cake

Ingredients:

1/4 cup self-rising flour
1/4 cup white sugar
1 egg, beaten
3 tbsps. cocoa powder
3 tbsps. chocolate-hazelnut spread (such as Nutella)
3 tbsps. milk
3 tbsps. vegetable oil

Directions:

1. Beat flour, sugar, egg, cocoa powder, chocolate-hazelnut spread, milk, and vegetable oil together in a large coffee mug with a fork until smooth.
2. Cook in microwave oven on high until cooked in the center, 90 seconds to 3 minutes.

Lemon Cake in a Mug

Ingredients:

6 tbsps. all-purpose flour
1/4 cup white sugar
1/8 tsp. baking powder
1 egg
3 tbsps. white sugar
1 tbsp. lemon juice

Directions:

1. Combine flour, 1/4 cup white sugar, and baking powder together in a mug.
2. Add egg, vegetable oil, water, and 1 tbsp. lemon juice; stir until well mixed.
3. Cook in the microwave on high until cake is cooked through, 2 1/2 to 3 minutes.
4. Remove from microwave and cool.
5. Mix 3 tbsps. white sugar and 1 tbsp. lemon juice together in a microwave-safe bowl until smooth; cook in microwave until sauce is bubbling, about 30 seconds.
6. Pour sauce over cake.

Peach Cobbler In a Mug

Ingredients:

1 tbsp. butter
2 tbsps. water
2 tbsps. all-purpose flour
1 tbsp. non-fat dry milk
1/8 tsp. baking powder
1/8 tsp. ground cinnamon
1 pinch salt
1 (4 oz.) container sliced peaches, well drained

Directions:

1. Melt butter in a mug in microwave, about 20 seconds.
2. Stir water, flour, dry milk, baking powder, ground cinnamon, and salt into butter until well blended.
3. Place peach slices on top of batter.
4. Microwave on 70% power until cooked through, about 2 minutes.
5. Let stand in microwave for 1 minute to set.

Banana Mug Cake

Ingredients:

3 tbsps. self-rising flour
2 tbsps. brown sugar
1 tbsp. white sugar
1 tsp. vanilla sugar
1 egg
1 tbsp. olive oil
1 tbsp. milk
1 ripe banana, mashed
3 crushed pecans, or more to taste

Directions:

1. Combine flour, brown sugar, white sugar, and vanilla sugar in a large microwave-safe mug.
2. Add egg and mix well.
3. Stir in oil, milk, mashed banana, and pecans.
4. Mix well to incorporate all the flour.
5. Microwave at high power until cake has risen and is cooked through, 2 1/2 to 3 minutes.
6. Remove and allow to cool slightly before eating.

Pumpkin Mug Cake

Ingredients:

6 tbsps. vanilla cake mix
2 tbsps. canned pumpkin puree
1 tsp. pumpkin pie spice
1 tbsp. milk
1 tbsp. vegetable oil
Whipped cream, for topping

Directions:

1. In a large mug, whisk (with a small whisk or large fork) together the cake mix, pumpkin puree, pumpkin pie spice, milk, and vegetable oil. Whisk until smooth.
2. Cook in the microwave on high for 1 minute and 30 seconds.
3. Top with whipped cream and extra cinnamon if you like.
4. Serve and enjoy!

Honey Mug Cake

Cake Ingredients:

2 tbsp. butter
2 tbsp. runny honey
1 egg
1/2 tsp. vanilla extract
3 tbsp. light brown sugar
4 tbsp. self-rising flour
1 pinch of salt

Frosting Ingredients:

2 tbsp. butter, softened
4 tbsp. confectioners' sugar
Runny honey

Directions:

1. Add the butter to a mug and melt in the microwave for around 10-20 seconds.
2. Add the honey, egg and vanilla and beat with a fork until combined.
3. Add the sugar, flour and salt and beat again until fully combined and smooth.
4. Cook in the microwave for around 1 minute 15 seconds to 1 minute 30 seconds (depending on your microwave power), then allow to cool to room temperature.
5. Meanwhile, to make the frosting, add the butter and confectioners' sugar to another mug and use a fork to cut the butter into the icing sugar until it reaches a clumpy texture, then beat with the fork until fluffy, around 1-2 minutes).
6. Spoon the frosting into a small piping bag or a ziplock bag fitted with an open star or plain round tip and pipe a swirl onto the top of the cooled cake.
7. Drizzle with extra honey and serve immediately.

Raspberry and White Chocolate Mug Muffin

Ingredients:

2 tbsp. unsalted butter, softened
3 tbsp. light brown sugar
1 medium egg
1 tbsp. milk
1 tsp. vanilla extract
pinch salt
4 tbsp. self-rising flour
3 tbsp. fresh raspberries
3 tbsp. white chocolate chips

Directions:

1. Add the butter to a mug and melt in the microwave for around 10-30 seconds.
2. Add the sugar, egg, milk, and vanilla and beat with a fork until well combined.
3. Stir in the salt and flour until the mixture starts to come together, then fold the raspberries and white chocolate chips until smooth.
4. Cook in the microwave for 1 minute 30 seconds or up to 2 minutes, depending on your microwave power.
5. Remove from the microwave and allow to cool for around 10-15 minutes before serving.
6. Serve and enjoy!

Chocolate Walnut Mug Cake

Ingredients:

3 tbsps. maple syrup
1 egg
1/4 tsp. vanilla extract
4 tbsps. all-purpose flour
1/4 tsp. baking powder
1 pinch salt
2 tbsps. chopped walnuts
1 tbsp. chocolate chips

Directions:

1. Whisk together maple syrup, egg, and vanilla extract in a large mug.
2. Mix flour, baking powder, and salt in a small bowl.
3. Stir into the maple syrup mixture until well combined.
4. Fold in walnuts and chocolate chips.
5. Microwave at the highest setting until mug cake has set and risen well, about 2 minutes.
6. Keep microwaving at 15-second intervals if it still appears soft.

Pineapple and Mint Mug Cake

Ingredients:

2 slices fresh pineapple
1 ripe banana
2 tbsps. cream of coconut
1 tbsp. rolled oats
1 tbsp. quick-cooking oats
1/4 tsp. baking powder
3 leaves fresh mint
1 tsp. chia seeds
1 tsp. poppy seeds

Directions:

1. Combine pineapple, banana, cream of coconut, rolled oats, quick-cooking oats, baking powder, mint, chia seeds, and poppy seeds in a blender; blend until smooth.
2. Pour into 2 mugs.
3. Microwave at the highest setting until mug cakes have set and risen well, about 3 minutes.
4. Allow to cool a few minutes before serving.

Red Velvet Mug Cake

Mug Cake Ingredients:

2 tbsp. buttermilk
1 tbsp. cider vinegar
1 1/2 tbsp. vegetable oil
red gel food coloring
2 tbsp. granulated sugar
1 tbsp. cocoa powder
pinch salt
pinch baking soda
4 tbsp. self-raising flour

Frosting Ingredients:

1 tbsp. unsalted butter, softened
1 tbsp. cream cheese, softened
4-5 tbsp. confectioners' sugar
1/2-1 tsp. milk, if needed
Sprinkles, optional

Directions:

1. To make the mug cake, add the wet ingredients (buttermilk, cider vinegar, vegetable oil and 2-5 drops of red food coloring) into a mug.
2. Add the sugar, salt and cocoa powder and whisk with a fork until smooth.
3. Fold in the flour and baking soda, and heat on full power in the microwave for between 1 minute to 1 minute 30 seconds, depending on the power of your microwave.
4. Check at 1 minute, and 1 minute 15 seconds.
5. The cake should be moist so if testing with a toothpick, some crumbs may cling.
6. Remove from the microwave and allow to cool fully before frosting. You can speed this up by popping in the fridge for around 30 minutes - 1 hour.
7. Once fully cooled make the cream cheese frosting by adding the butter and cream cheese to a clean mug and beat with a clean fork until softened further.
8. Gradually add in the icing sugar, beating after each addition. You may not need to add in the milk, so only add if needed.
9. Spoon or pipe the frosting over the cooled cake and sprinkle on some sprinkles, if desired.
10. Serve and enjoy!

Gingerbread Mug Cake

Cake Ingredients:

2 tbsp. unsalted butter
3 tbsp. light brown sugar
1 egg
1 tbsp. molasses
1/4 tsp. vanilla
1 pinch of salt
4 tbsp. all-purpose flour
1/4 tsp. baking powder
1/2 tsp. ground ginger
1/8 tsp. cinnamon
small pinch of cloves, optional

Frosting Ingredients:

3 tbsp. unsalted butter, softened
8-10 tbsp. powdered sugar, sifted
1/4-1/2 tsp. milk, optional

Directions:

1. To make the mug cake, add the butter to a large mug and microwave on high for 20-30 seconds, or until melted.
2. Add the light brown sugar and beat with a fork until smooth.
3. Add the egg, molasses, vanilla, and salt and beat again until smooth and fully combined.
4. Sift in the flour, baking powder, and spices, and carefully stir until smooth.
5. Cook in the microwave for around 1 minute 30 seconds (800W). Depending on your microwave's power, it may take anywhere from 1 minute to 1 minute 45 seconds. The cake will spring back to the touch when ready.
6. Allow to cool completely if frosting. Or allow to cool for 10-15 minutes if enjoying warm.
7. To make the frosting, add the butter to a clean mug and whisk until softened.
8. Add the powered sugar, a tbsp. at a time, until the correct consistency is reached. Whisk in the milk and add more powdered sugar, if necessary.
9. Pipe or spread over the cooled mug cake and decorate with sprinkles, if desired.

Vanilla Bean Mug Cake

Cake Ingredients:

3 tbsps. flour
1.5 tbsps. sugar
1/8-1/4 tsp. baking powder (a scant 1/4 tsp.)
pinch of salt
3 tbsps. milk
1/2 tsp. vanilla bean paste
1 tbsp. melted butter

Frosting Ingredients:

1 1/2 tbsp. room temp cream cheese
2 tbsps. powdered sugar
1/4 tsp. vanilla bean paste

Directions:

1. In a small mug or ramekin, mix the dry cake ingredients well.
2. Add the milk, vanilla paste, and butter, then mix until just combined.
3. Microwave cake for 1 minute.
4. When the cake is done, it will pull away from the mug a little bit.
5. Mix the frosting ingredients then top cake with frosting.

Microwave Ginger Mug Cake

Ingredients:

1 tbsp. butter
1 egg
1 tbsp. brown sugar
1 tbsp. white sugar
2 tsps. molasses
1/2 tsp. vanilla extract
3 tbsps. whole wheat flour
2 tbsps. wheat germ
1/2 tsp. ground ginger
1/4 tsp. ground cinnamon
1/8 tsp. baking soda
1 pinch salt

Icing Ingredients:

3 tbsps. confectioners' sugar
1 1/2 tsps. water

Directions:

1. Place butter in a microwave-safe mug. Heat in the microwave until melted, 10 to 20 seconds. Whisk in egg, brown sugar, white sugar, molasses, and vanilla extract.
2. Mix whole wheat flour, wheat germ, ginger, cinnamon, baking soda, and salt together in a small bowl.
3. Add to the mug; stir well until combined.
4. Cook in the microwave in 40-second intervals until the top springs back when lightly pressed, about 1 minute 20 seconds.
5. Whisk confectioners' sugar and water together in a small bowl to make icing.
6. Invert cake onto a serving plate and drizzle icing on top.

Cookies and Cream Mug Cake

Ingredients:

1/4 cup white chocolate chips
3 tbsp. whole milk
4 tbsp. all-purpose flour
1/4 tsp. baking powder
1/2 tbsp. vegetable oil
2 Oreo cookies

Directions:

1. Combine white chocolate chips and milk in an oversized microwave-safe mug. Microwave for about 40 seconds.
2. Mix with a small whisk until chocolate is completely melted.
3. Add flour, baking powder, and oil and whisk until batter is smooth.
4. Using a fork, smash Oreos into the batter until only small chunks of cookie remain.
5. Cook in microwave for about 1 minute.
6. Let cake cool a few minutes before eating.
7. Serve and enjoy!

Carrot Cake Mug Cake

Ingredients:

Mug Cake
1/4 cup flour
2 tbsp. brown sugar
1/4 tsp. cinnamon
1/8 tsp. nutmeg
1 tbsp. butter melted
2 tbsp. carrots shredded
1/4 tsp. baking powder
1/4 cup milk
Toppings
Whipped cream
Chopped pecans
Shredded carrots

Directions:

1. In a large mug, combine all ingredients in and stir until there are no lumps.
2. Microwave for 1-1.5 minutes or until baked through.
3. Top with whipped cream, chopped pecans, and shredded carrots.
4. Serve and enjoy!

Dulce de Leche Mug Cake

Ingredients:

3 tbsp. coconut flour
1/4 tsp. baking powder
4 tbsp. coconut milk
1/2 medium ripe banana, mashed
1 tbsp. dulce de leche, plus more for topping
1/2 tsp. vanilla extract

Directions:

1. In a small bowl, add the flour and baking powder.
2. Mix well until combined.
3. Add all the remaining ingredients and stir until mixed well.
4. Pour the mixture into 2 small mugs.
5. Microwave them for about 2-3mins. The time will depend on the power of the microwave and the thickness of the mug.
6. Remove from the Microwave and top the cakes with a little bit of dulce de leche.
7. Let them cool down for about 2 minutes before serving.

Dark Chocolate Espresso Mug Cake

Ingredients:

4 oz. dark chocolate chips
1 tbsp. coconut oil
2 tbsps. water
1 tbsp. blanched almond flour
1 tbsp. coconut flour
1 pinch baking soda
1 egg
1 tbsp. brewed espresso

Directions:

1. Combine chocolate chips and coconut oil in a microwave-safe mug; heat in the microwave until melted, about 30 seconds.
2. Whisk water, almond flour, coconut flour, and baking soda into the chocolate mixture until well combined.
3. Add egg and brewed espresso; whisk until smooth.
4. Heat in the microwave until cake is cooked through, about 90 seconds. Let cool before serving, about 2 minutes.

Mug Sponge Cake

Ingredients:

2 tbsps. butter
1 large egg
2 tbsps. milk
1 tsp. pure vanilla extract
1 tsp. almond extract, optional
1/4 cup granulated sugar
6 tbsps. flour
1/4 tsp. baking powder
1 pinch of salt

Directions:

1. Place the butter in a large mug and microwave it for 20 to 30 seconds until melted.
2. Add the egg and whisk it in with a fork.
3. Stir in the milk, vanilla, almond and sugar.
4. Add the flour, baking powder and salt.
5. Mix the batter with a fork until smooth.
6. Cover and place in the fridge. When ready to serve microwave for 1 minute and 20 seconds.
7. Top with whipped cream and fresh berries and enjoy!

Peanut Butter Cookie in a Mug

Ingredients:

1 tbsp. butter
1 tbsp. peanut butter
1 tbsp. brown sugar
1 tbsp. white sugar
1 pinch salt
1 egg
3 tbsps. all-purpose flour

Directions:

1. Place butter and peanut butter in a microwave-safe mug.
2. Microwave until butter and peanut butter are melted, about 30 seconds.
3. Stir brown sugar, white sugar, and salt into butter mixture.
4. Add egg; stir flour into mixture.
5. Cook in the microwave until cookie is set, 2 to 4 minutes.

Microwave Mug Apple Crisp

Ingredients:

3 tbsps. butter, melted
4 tbsps. oats
2 tbsps. chopped pecans
2 tbsps. all-purpose flour
2 tbsps. brown sugar
1/4 tsp. cinnamon
1/8 tsp. salt
1 small apple , peeled diced
1/2 tbsp. all-purpose flour
1/2 tbsp. brown sugar
1/4 tsp. cinnamon

Directions:

1. In a small bowl stir in the oats, flour, pecans, brown sugar, cinnamon, and the salt.
2. Stir in the melted butter to create the crisp topping
3. Chop the apples small and toss them with the 1/2 tbsp. of flour, 1/2 tbsp. of the sugar, and ¼ tsp. cinnamon.
4. Take a Microwaveable mug and fill with the apple. You can fill the mug because the apples cook down.
5. Spoon the crisp mixture over the top.
6. Microwave for 2- 2 1/2 minutes. the apples should be bubbling and the whole thing will reduce in size.
7. Carefully remove from the microwave and let stand until cool enough to eat.
8. Enjoy warm with vanilla ice cream

Mug Brownie

Ingredients:

3 tbsps. all-purpose flour
3 tbsps. brown sugar
3 tbsps. cocoa powder
3 tbsps. flavorless oil (canola oil/coconut oil/sunflower oil)
3 tbsps. water
1 pinch of salt
1/2 tsp. vanilla extract
2 tsps. chocolate chips

Directions:

1. In a microwavable mug mix together all the ingredients.
2. Mix in the chocolate chips.
3. If you don't want to cook them off straight away, then place them in the refrigerator for up to 24 hours.
4. Microwave for 45-60 seconds.
5. Allow to cool for at least 5 minutes.
6. Serve warm with vanilla ice cream & enjoy!

Microwave Mug Blondie

Ingredients:

2 tbsps. butter, melted
3 tbsps. brown sugar
3 tbsps. milk
½ tsp. vanilla
6 tbsps. flour
1/8 tsp. salt
1/8 tsp. baking powder
1 tbsp. white chocolate chips
4 caramel candies , chopped
Ice cream and caramel sauce for topping (optional)

Directions:

1. Melt butter in a large, microwave-safe mug,
2. Add the brown sugar, milk and vanilla and mix until the sugar is dissolved
3. Gradually stir in flour, salt and baking powder.
4. Stir until well-blended.
5. Add the white chocolate chips and caramel candies.
6. Cover and store in the fridge for up to 2 days. When ready to eat, microwave for 1 minute and 20 seconds. If the batter looks a bit undercooked microwave for an additional 30 seconds until cooked.
7. Top with ice cream and caramel sauce and enjoy!

Cinnamon Roll in a Mug

Ingredients:

For the cinnamon roll
9 level tbsps. all-purpose flour
3/4 tsp. baking powder
a pinch of salt
3-4 1/2 tbsps. water
1 dab vegetable oil for greasing the mug
3/4 tsp. cinnamon
1 1/2 tbsps. coconut sugar
1/2 tsp. water
For the frosting
3 tbsps. powdered sugar
3/4 tsp. milk or water

Frosting Directions:

1. In a small bowl mix the powdered sugar with either milk or water.
2. Add the liquid a tiny bit at a time.
3. Stir well until smooth then set aside.

Directions:

1. Grease a normal sized drinking mug with a dab of oil.
4. Add the flour, baking powder and salt to another small bowl and stir to combine.
5. Gradually add the water (from the 3-4½ tbsps.), stirring until it starts to form a dough then use your hand to bring it together, kneading a few times until it's a smooth, flexible ball of dough.
6. If you do accidentally add a drop too much water and it's a bit sticky, add a little tiny bit more flour.
7. Dust work surface with flour and roll the dough out into a long strip about 4 inches wide and a couple of millimeters thick
8. Sprinkle the coconut sugar and cinnamon evenly over the dough then fold the edges inwards to seal it in and stop it all falling out when you lift it into the mug.
9. It should be a long narrow strip which you can roll up.
10. Roll it up and gently lift it and place it in the greased mug.
11. Pour 1/2 tsp. over water then place in the microwave.
12. Microwave uncovered on full power for 45-50 seconds.
13. A toothpick inserted into the dough it should come out clean.
14. Add the frosting.
15. Serve and enjoy!

Blueberry Muffin in a Mug

Ingredients:

3 tbsps. whole wheat flour
1 tbsp. old-fashioned rolled oats
1/4 tsp. baking soda
1/4 tsp. ground cinnamon
1 pinch ground cloves
1 pinch ground nutmeg
1 pinch baking powder
1 pinch salt
1 egg white
1 tbsp. milk, or more as needed
1 tbsp. brown sugar, or more to taste
1/2 tsp. vanilla extract
1/2 cup fresh blueberries

Directions:

1. Mix flour, oats, baking soda, cinnamon, cloves, nutmeg, baking powder, and salt together in a microwave-safe mug.
2. Stir egg white, milk, brown sugar, and vanilla extract into flour mixture until batter is fully combined; slowly stir in blueberries.
3. Cook in microwave for 1 minute.
4. Check muffin for doneness and continue cooking in 15 second increments until cooked through, about 1 minute more.

Monkey Bread in a Mug

Dough Ingredients:

2 1/2 tbsps. all-purpose flour, or more if needed
1/2 tsp. baking powder
3/4 tbsp. milk
1 tbsp. white sugar
1/4 tsp. ground cinnamon

Sauce Ingredients:

2 tbsps. butter
1 1/2 tbsps. brown sugar
1 tsp. ground cinnamon

Directions:

1. Grease a microwave-safe mug.
2. Mix flour, butter, and baking powder in a bowl with a fork until crumbly.
3. Add milk and knead into a dough, adding more flour if dough is too sticky.
4. Place 1 tbsp. butter in a small microwave-safe bowl.
5. Heat until melted, about 10 seconds.
6. Mix white sugar and 1/4 tsp. cinnamon together in a small bowl to make cinnamon sugar.
7. Break off quarter-size balls of dough.
8. Dip each ball in melted butter; coat with cinnamon sugar.
9. Place dough balls into prepared mug.
10. Place 2 tbsps. butter in a small microwave-safe bowl.
11. Heat until melted, about 20 seconds.
12. Stir in brown sugar and 1 tsp. cinnamon.
13. Drizzle over dough balls. Microwave until golden brown, about 1 minute.
14. Let cool before serving.

Mug Peach Cobbler

Ingredients:

1 tbsp. butter
2 tbsps. water
2 tbsps. all-purpose flour
1 tbsp. dry milk
1/8 tsp. baking powder
1/8 tsp. ground cinnamon
1 pinch salt
1 (4 oz.) container sliced peaches, well drained

Directions:

1. Melt butter in a mug in microwave, about 20 seconds.
2. Stir water, flour, dry milk, baking powder, ground cinnamon, and salt into butter until well blended.
3. Place peach slices on top of batter.
4. Microwave on 70% power until cooked through, about 2 minutes. Let stand in microwave for 1 minute to set.

Mug French Toast

Ingredients:

2 slices bread
1 egg
3 tbsps. milk
1 dash of cinnamon

Directions:

1. Cube slices of bread.
2. Place bread cubes in mug.
3. Combine egg, milk and cinnamon in a separate small bowl.
4. Pour egg mixture into mug.
5. Press bread down so it can fully absorb liquid.
6. Microwave for one minute, and then ten seconds at a time until fully cooked.

Mug S'mores

Ingredients:

1 tsp. butter
1/2 graham cracker sheet
2 tbsps. milk
1 tbsp. + 2 tsps. oil
2 1/2 tbsps. white sugar
2 1/2 tbsps. unsweetened cocoa powder
3 tbsps. flour
1/4 tsp. baking powder
Part of a milk chocolate bar, broken into small chunks
1-3 large marshmallows

Directions:

1. Melt butter in a glass bowl.
2. Crumble graham cracker sheet and mix in to melted butter. Set aside.
3. Mix wet ingredients in a microwaveable mug, then add the dry ingredients and mix together.
4. Fold in chocolate chunks.
5. Make an indentation in the middle of the batter and press the graham cracker mixture into the sides of the indentation.
6. Put a whole marshmallow into the center of the spot you've created. Push it down—the marshmallow will expand as it is heated. Then sprinkle chocolate chunks and graham cracker crumbs to top it off!
7. Microwave for 40 seconds.
8. Cut/tear remaining marshmallow(s) into smaller pieces and push into the top of the cake.
9. Microwave an additional 30 seconds. Let sit in the microwave to cool a bit, then study snack away.

S'mores Dip

Ingredients:

Non-stick cooking spray
1/2 cup graham cracker crumbs
2 tsp. unsalted butter, melted
2 tbsp. semi-sweet chocolate chips
2 tbsp. mini marshmallows
1/8 tsp. ground cinnamon
6 large strawberries, for dipping

Directions:

1. Spray mug with cooking spray.
2. Add the graham cracker crumbs and butter, mix, and pat down with a spoon.
3. Add the chocolate chips and then the marshmallows.
4. Cover and microwave until the marshmallows and chips melt, about 1 minute.
5. Sprinkle with the cinnamon and serve with the whole strawberries for dipping.

Mug Nachos

Ingredients:

Nonstick cooking spray
1/2 cup canned refried beans
3 tbsp. salsa
10 tortilla chips, or more if desired
3 tbsp. shredded Mexican cheese blend
1/2 avocado, diced
1 tsp. sour cream, for garnish (optional)
1 tsp. canned green chilis, for garnish (optional)
1 tsp. thinly sliced trimmed scallions, for garnish (optional)

Directions:

1. Spray the inside of a 12-oz. mug with cooking spray.
2. In a small bowl, stir together the beans and salsa.
3. Place half of the chips in the mug and top with a third of the cheese and half of the bean-salsa mixture.
4. Top with the remaining chips, another third of the cheese, and the remaining bean mixture.
5. Top with the remaining cheese.
6. Cover and microwave until most of the cheese melts, about 1 minute.
7. Uncover and microwave until the remainder of the cheese melts, about another 30 seconds.
8. Top with the avocado and other garnishes, and serve with additional chips, if desired.

Banana Nut Bread in a Mug

Ingredients:

3 tbsp. flour
1 1/2 tbsp. sugar
1 egg
1/4 tsp. vanilla extract
3/4 tbsp. vegetable oil
1 tbsp. milk
1 ripe banana, mashed
1 pinch of salt
1 pinch of baking powder
1 pinch of baking soda
Non-Stick baking spray or some butter to coat the mug
Nutella, walnuts, peanut butter, cookie butter, chocolate chips (optional)

Directions:

1. Whisk together dry ingredients directly into a mug.
2. Add in the egg and stir until thoroughly combined.
3. Mix in the rest of the ingredients.
4. Microwave for 2 1/2 to 3 minutes at 60-second intervals.
5. Serve and enjoy!

Flaxseed Oatmeal in a Mug

Ingredients:

1/3 cup rolled oats
1/2 cup milk
1/2 tbsp. chia seeds
1 tbsp. flaxseed meal
1 tbsp. nut butter
Cinnamon, to taste
Honey, to taste
Pepitas, nuts and fruit as toppings

Directions:

1. Using a microwave-safe bowl, add in the oats, milk and chia seeds.
2. Microwave on regular for 3-4 minutes (3 minutes gives you a chewier oats; whichever you prefer).
3. Add flaxseed meal, a little extra milk if you prefer, honey, cinnamon, nut butter and whatever toppings you want.
4. Serve and enjoy!

Banana Nut Oatmeal in a Mug

Ingredients:

1/2 banana, sliced
1/3 cup rolled oats
1/2 cup milk
1/2 tbsp. chia seeds
1 tbsp. flaxseed meal
1 tbsp. nut butter
Cinnamon, to taste
Nuts as toppings

Directions:

1. Using a microwave-safe bowl, add in the oats, milk, banana and chia seeds.
2. Microwave for 3-4 minutes (3 minutes gives you a chewier oats).
3. Add flaxseed meal, a little extra milk, cinnamon, nut butter and nuts for toppings.
4. Serve and enjoy!

Chocoholic Oatmeal in a Mug

Ingredients:

1/3 cup rolled oats
1/2 cup milk
1 tbsp. flaxseed meal
1/2 tbsp. cocoa powder
1 tbsp. dark chocolate chips
Nuts

Directions:

1. Using a microwave-safe bowl, add in the oats, milk and cocoa powder.
2. Microwave on regular for 3-4 minutes (3 minutes gives you a chewier oats; whichever you prefer).
3. Add flaxseed meal, a little extra milk if you prefer.
4. Add chocolate chips and nuts.
5. Serve and enjoy!

Tropical Sunrise Oatmeal in a Mug

Ingredients:

1/3 cup rolled oats
1/2 cup milk
1/2 tbsp. chia seeds
1 tbsp. flaxseed meal
Cinnamon, to taste
1/2 tbsp. coconut oil
Honey, to taste
Pepitas
Nuts
Dried mango
Pineapple

Directions:

1. Using a microwave-safe bowl, add in the oats, milk, coconut oil and chia seeds.
2. Microwave on regular for 3-4 minutes (3 minutes gives you a chewier oats; whichever you prefer).
3. Add flaxseed meal, a little extra milk, honey, cinnamon, mango and pineapple.
4. Serve and enjoy!

Mug Pumpkin Pie

Ingredients:

2 tbsps. crushed cracker cookie crumbs
1/3 cup pumpkin puree
1 egg
1 tbsp. milk
2 tbsps. brown sugar
1 tsp. pumpkin pie spice
1 generous pinch of salt
1/2 tsp. vanilla

Directions:

1. In a small bowl, whisk together the pumpkin puree, egg, milk, brown sugar, pumpkin pie spice and salt until no lumps
2. In a microwavable mug add in your crushed cookies to the bottom.
3. Pour into your pumpkin pie mix on top
4. Microwave roughly 1 1/2 -2 minutes, checking every 30 seconds.
5. The top may look slightly damp but it will set as it cools.
6. Carefully remove the mug from the microwave.
7. Let it stand for a couple minutes to cool.
8. Serve with whipped cream and enjoy!

Mug Pecan Pie

Ingredients:

1 1/2 tbsp. butter, melted
2/3 cups brown sugar
3 tbsp. maple syrup, honey or golden syrup
1 tsp. vanilla
1/8 tsp. salt
1 egg
2/3 cup pecans, chopped and toasted
2 graham crackers, crushed into 2 tbsps. of crumbs
Extra pecans for decoration

Directions:

1. In a small bowl, whisk together the butter, brown sugar, maple syrup, vanilla and salt.
2. Whisk in eggs.
3. In a microwavable mug add in your crushed cookies to the bottom.
4. Pour in your pecan pie mix.
5. Microwave roughly for 1- 1/2 minutes, checking every 30 seconds.
6. The mix will thicken and appear jelly like, but it will set as it cools.
7. Carefully remove the mug from the microwave.
8. Let it stand for a couple minutes to cool.
9. Serve with whipped cream and enjoy!

Brownie In a Mug

Ingredients:

1/4 cup white sugar
1/4 cup all-purpose flour
2 tbsps. cocoa powder
1 pinch salt
3 tbsps. water
2 tbsps. olive oil

Directions:

1. Stir sugar, flour, cocoa powder, and salt together in a mug.
2. Add water and olive oil; stir until mixture is evenly moist.
3. Cook in microwave for 1 minute 40 seconds.
4. Serve topped with ice cream.

Jelly Donut in a Mug

Ingredients:

2 tbsps. butter
4 tbsps. all-purpose flour
1 Egg yolk
2 tbsps. sugar
1 tbsp. milk
1/2 tsp. baking powder
1/4 tsp. ground cinnamon
1 tbsp. strawberry jam
Cinnamon sugar to garnish

Directions:

1. Place butter into a microwavable mug and microwave until just melted. (roughly 20 seconds)
2. Add in the remaining ingredients.
3. Mix well with fork until just combined.
4. Once the batter is mixed place the spoonful of jam down into the batter.
5. Microwave for 45 seconds or until is firm on top.
6. Always keep a close eye on your mug while in the microwave so it doesn't over flow or over cook.
7. Sprinkle some cinnamon sugar on top and enjoy straight away!

Mug Pizza

Ingredients:

4 tbsps. all-purpose flour
1/8 tsp. baking powder
1/16 tsp. baking soda
1/8 tsp. salt
3 tbsps. milk
1 tbsp. olive oil
1 tbsp. marinara sauce
1 generous tbsp. shredded mozzarella cheese
5 mini pepperoni
1/2 tsp. dried Italian herbs (basil, oregano, etc.)

Directions:

1. Mix the flour, baking powder, baking soda and salt together in a microwavable mug
2. Add in the milk and oil with mix together.
3. There may be some lump but that is ok
4. Spoon on the marinara sauce and spread it around the surface of the batter
5. Sprinkle on the cheese, pepperoni and dried herbs
6. Microwave for 1 minute 10-20 seconds, or until it rises up and the topping are bubbling.
7. Serve and enjoy!

Mug Chili

Ingredients:

3 tbsps. red kidney beans
3 tbsps. corn
3 tbsps. carrots, finely chopped
1 tbsps. onion, finely chopped
6 tbsps. canned tomato or tomato sauce
1/2 tsp. cumin
1/2 tsp. chili powder
1 tsp. worcestershire sauce (optional)
1/2 tsp. dried chili or tabasco sauce

Directions:

1. In a medium sized microwaveable mug, combine all of your ingredients.
2. Cover with cling wrap and store in the fridge for up to 3 days.
3. When ready to eat remove the cling wrap and microwave for 2 to 2 1/2 minutes. This is just to heat through all ingredients.
4. Serve topped with sour cream, avocado and chopped green onion.

Mug Potato Soup

Ingredients:

3/4 cup water
3 tbsps. potatoes, in small cubes
1 tbsp. white onion, chopped
2 tbsps. cheddar cheese
1 tbsp. bacon, cooked
2 tsp. cornstarch
1/2 cup chicken stock (or vegetable stock)
1/4 cup milk
Salt and pepper to taste
Sour cream for garnish, optional

Directions:

1. Add your potatoes and water into a large microwaveable mug. Microwave for 3-4 min or until the potatoes are tender. Check on it half way through and stir
2. Once cooked drain away the cooking water
3. Into the potatoes stir in the bacon, cheese and onions and cornflour. The cornflour will thicken your soup.
4. Stir in the stock and milk and season with salt and pepper
5. Place in the microwave and cook for 2 1/2 - 3 minutes or until it thickens and all of your ingredients have heated through. (Cooking time is based on my 1200W microwave so your timing might vary) Always keep a close eye on your mug while in the microwave so it doesn't over flow or over cook.
6. Serve topped with sour cream and some more sprinkles of bacon and chives

Egg MugMuffin

Ingredients:

5 tbsps. all-purpose flour
1/4 tsp. baking powder
1/8 tsp. baking soda
1/8 tsp. salt
2 tbsps. milk
2 tsps. vegetable oil or melted butter
2 tbsps. egg
1 tbsp. grated cheddar cheese
1 tbsp. scallions, chopped
1 egg

Directions:

1. In a large microwave safe mug mix together the flour, baking powder, baking soda and salt with a fork.
2. Add in the milk, oil, egg, cheese and scallions and mix together until just combined.
3. Make a well in the center of the batter with a spoon and crack in your egg into the center.
4. Spoon the batter from the sides over the top of the egg.
5. Place in the microwave and cook for 50 seconds- 1 minute 10 seconds.
6. It is cooked when it is firm to the touch on top.
7. Watch closely while in the microwave so it doesn't over flow or over cook.
8. Serve and enjoy!

Scrambled Eggs in a Mug

Ingredients:

1 egg
1 tbsp. milk
1 pinch ground black pepper (optional)

Directions:

1. Crack egg into a microwave-safe mug; beat until even in color.
2. Pour in milk and beat until light yellow in color.
3. Heat in microwave until cooked through and fluffy, about 90 seconds.
4. Sprinkle pepper over egg.

Omelette in a Mug

Ingredients:

1 large egg
2 egg whites
2 tbsps. shredded cheddar cheese
2 tbsps. diced fully cooked ham
1 tbsp. diced green bell pepper
salt and ground black pepper to taste
cooking spray

Directions:

1. Combine egg, egg whites, cheddar cheese, ham, bell pepper, salt, and ground pepper in a microwave-safe mug coated with non-stick spray.
2. Microwave on high for 1 minute; stir. Return to microwave and cook until eggs are completely set, 1 to 1 1/2 minutes longer.

Burrito in a Mug

Ingredients:

1 large 9 inch tortilla
2 eggs
2 tbsps. beans (pinto or black beans)
2 tbsps. cheddar cheese , grated
2 tbsps. scallions, chopped
Salt and pepper to taste
Salsa or sour cream for garnish

Directions:

1. In a large microwavable mug press in a fresh tortilla. It will naturally fold into the shape of the mug and find its way.
2. Crack in your eggs and whisk up with a fork, taking care not to tear the tortilla.
3. Add in your favorite burrito items like cheese, beans and scallions.
4. Season with salt and pepper and mix all together.
5. Microwave for 1 minute 20 seconds.
6. Check, and if the eggs are still liquid, cook for another 15 -20 seconds.
7. Keep an eye during cooking so the eggs don't over heat.
8. Once done, let it sit for 3 minutes to cool.
9. Serve with some sour cream and salsa on top.

Omelet in a Mug

Ingredients:

1 large egg
2 egg whites
2 tbsps. shredded Cheddar cheese
1 tbsp. diced green bell pepper
Salt and ground black pepper to taste
Cooking spray
2 tbsps. diced fully cooked ham

Directions:

1. Combine egg, egg whites, Cheddar cheese, ham, bell pepper, salt, and ground pepper in a microwave-safe mug coated with non-stick spray.
2. Microwave on high for 1 minute; stir. Return to microwave and cook until eggs are completely set, 1 to 1 1/2 minutes longer.

Meatloaf in a Mug

Ingredients:

1 slice white bread, torn into pieces
2 tbsps. milk
1/2 tsp. Worcestershire sauce
1/4 pound ground beef
1 green onion, thinly sliced
1/4 tsp. seasoned salt
1/8 tsp. ground black pepper

Directions:

1. Place the torn bread into a small bowl, and pour in the milk and Worcestershire sauce; set aside for a few minutes for the bread to absorb the liquid.
2. Add the ground beef, green onion, seasoned salt, and pepper to the bread; mix well and place into a 10 oz., microwave-safe mug.
3. Cook in the microwave at 70 percent power until the meatloaf is firm and no longer pink in the center, 4 to 5 1/2 minutes depending on the microwave.
4. Remove the meatloaf from the microwave, and allow to stand 2 minutes before serving.

Chicken Pot Pie in a Mug

Ingredients:

3-4 tbsps. cooked chicken
2 tbsps. frozen vegetables (peas and carrots)
1 1/2 tsps. cornstarch
Salt and pepper
3 tbsps. chicken stock
/8 tsp. salt
1/2 tbsp. butter, cubed
3 1/2 tbsps. milk (or buttermilk)
1 tbsp. chopped herbs

Directions:

1. In a large microwavable mug add in the cooked chicken, frozen vegetables, cornstarch, salt and pepper.
2. Stir well together to mix in the cornstarch.
3. Pour in the stock and milk and stir well until everything is combined. Set aside.
4. For the biscuit topping: Mix together the flour, baking powder and salt.
5. Using a fork rub in the cubed butter into the dry ingredients. When done it will resemble fine breadcrumbs.
6. Stir in the milk and herbs until your mix forms a batter. (I decided to leave out the cheese for the pie topping).
7. Gently scoop the batter on top of the chicken pie mix.
8. It might sink a little, don't worry that is fine. During cooking it will rise up.
9. Microwave for roughly 2 minutes- 2 minutes 15 seconds. It is ready when the biscuit batter is firm on top and you don't see any wet batter.
10. Serve and enjoy!

About the Author

Laura Sommers is **The Recipe Lady!**

She is a loving wife and mother who lives on a small farm in Baltimore County, Maryland and has a passion for all things domestic especially when it comes to saving money. She has a profitable eBay business and is a couponing addict. Follow her tips and tricks to learn how to make delicious meals on a budget, save money or to learn the latest life hack!

Visit her Amazon Author Page to see her latest books:

amazon.com/author/laurasommers

Visit the Recipe Lady's blog for even more great recipes:

http://the-recipe-lady.blogspot.com/

Follow the Recipe Lady on **Pinterest**:

http://pinterest.com/therecipelady1

Other Books by Laura Sommers

- Recipe Hacks for Beer
- Recipe Hacks for Potato Chips
- Recipe Hacks for a Bottle of Italian Salad Dressing
- Recipe Hacks for Dry Onion Soup Mix
- Recipe Hacks for Cheese Puffs
- Recipe Hacks for Pasta Sauce
- Recipe Hacks for Dry Vegetable Soup Mix
- Recipe Hacks for Canned Tuna Fish
- Recipe Hacks for Saltine Crackers
- Recipe Hacks for Pancake Mix
- Recipe Hacks for Instant Mashed Potato Flakes
- Recipe Hacks for Sriracha Hot Chili Sauce
- Recipe Hacks for Dry Ranch Salad Dressing and Dip Mix
- Recipe Hacks for Canned Biscuits
- Recipe Hacks for Canned Soup
- Recipe Hacks for Oreo Cookies
- Recipe Hacks for a Box of Mac & Cheese

May all of your meals be a banquet
with good friends and good food.

Made in the USA
Columbia, SC
17 June 2020